**Illustrated by**
Sue Gibson
Ian Jackson
Steve Kaye

**Cover illustration**
Richard Orr

## Acknowledgements
**BRUCE COLEMAN**: title page (M P Kahl); 8U (H Albrecht); 9B (G Bingham); 10C (Dr E Pott); 11U (R Wilmshurst); 19U (M P Kahl); 30U (F Saver); 33U (R Schroeder). **FRANK LANE**: 14B (C Carvalho); 28U (M Newman); 31U (R Thompson); 35B (W Wisniewski). **NHPA**: 10U (B Hawkes); 11B (L H Newman); 23U (P Fagot); 29U (A Bannister); 34C (M W F Tweedie); 36U (G I Bernard). **OXFORD SCIENTIFIC**: 16U (D Allan). **SEAPHOT**: 10B (K Amsler). **SURVIVAL ANGLIA**: 11C (A Root); 12U (C Willock); 13U (D & M Plage); 15B (J & D Bartlett); 21U (B Davidson); 24U (J & D Bartlett); 32U (J Foott).

ISBN 1 85854 142 5

Published by Brimax Books Ltd, Newmarket, England 1994
Printed in Spain

# Safety in Numbers

Written by
Karen O'Callaghan & Kate Londesborough

BRIMAX · NEWMARKET · ENGLAND

# Contents

# Animals together

Animals that live together can help and protect each other.

Canada geese

baboons

polar bears

rattlesnakes

When more than two animals stay together, this is called a group. Some spend their lives in this way, while others form groups at special times of the year.

# Living in groups

Animals live together in large or small groups. These groups all have different names.

**Chimpanzee** groups are called clans. They live in the trees and on the ground. Males sometimes move to live with other clans.

**Mandrills** live in a group called a troop. The males have bright red and blue faces. They live together in the forest.

**Beavers** live in a small group called a family — mother, father and babies. The young that were born the year before may also still live with them.

Groups of **kangaroos** are called mobs. Several mobs may join together when they are resting in the shade.

Female **seals** form special groups called harems. One male seal lives with a harem of many female seals.

Soon after these baby seals are born their mothers go back to the sea. The pups live in a group called a pod. The mothers return to the pups to feed them.

These **snapper fish** swim together in groups called schools. They swim close together in the open sea.

Sea birds gather together in groups called colonies. These **gannets** nest together high up in the safety of the cliffs.

Several hundred thousand **flamingoes** also form a huge colony. On the shores of a lake they build nests for their young.

Many bird groups are called flocks. There may be a million birds in a flock of wild **budgerigars.**

# Many animals that live in the grasslands of Africa form very large groups called herds.

The **hippopotamus** likes to wallow in mud. At night, the herd leaves the river to look for food on the river bank.

**Ostriches** are always on the move. They live in large herds. They split into family groups during the rainy season.

**Buffalo** like to cover themselves with mud. This keeps them cool. It also keeps biting insects away. When the herd moves, young males gather in a special bachelor herd that follows behind the others.

Some **antelopes** form special nursery herds. These are groups of mothers and babies. The males go off to live by themselves.

# Leaving the group

The males in some family groups leave to live alone, while the females stay with their young. The male tiger and polar bear both leave their families.

Animals that hunt in teams are usually able to catch their prey, but the lone **tiger** has a harder time to find food.

The male **polar bear** rules the pack ice because it has no enemies. It is a fierce hunter and does not need the safety of a group.

# Safety in numbers

By staying together in a group, animals can help and protect each other in many ways.

When **giraffes** are feeding, each animal in the group faces in a different direction. In this way, they can look all around for an approaching lion.

When they are drinking, giraffes spread out their front legs and bend down to the water. In this position they cannot see behind them. The giraffes take turns to drink while others watch out for danger.

Penguin groups are called rookeries. These **Emperor penguins** help each other in the cold. The group huddles together with the chicks in the middle. Each adult rests its beak on the body of the bird in front. Packed tightly together, only a small part of their bodies faces the freezing winds, so they can keep warm.

**Musk oxen** are often attacked by **wolves** hunting in packs. They cannot outrun the wolves and there is nowhere to hide. The oxen form a circle around the babies. Facing outwards they use their huge curved horns to protect them. The wolves may be speared by the horns, or thrown backwards among the herd and trampled to death.

If **starlings** fly close together they can escape from an enemy. A **falcon** will not attack a flock of birds as it might crash into the flock and hurt itself.

When travelling in search of food, a **baboon** troop stays close together. The mothers and babies walk in the middle surrounded by the strong males. The troop can often scare away an enemy. Under attack, the baboons bare their teeth, make loud screeching noises, and bang and stamp on the ground. This can frighten even a fierce **leopard**.

# Signs and signals

Groups of animals need to be able to 'talk' to each other. To do this, they use signs, signals, noises and smells.

Every year **snow geese** set off on long journeys to new feeding grounds. They call out to each other, making loud honking noises when they are ready to leave. They also call out as they fly, to keep the flock together.

These **gazelles** use a signal. If one of the gazelles sees a **cheetah** it flares out the white hairs under its tail. Animals on the edge of the herd see this and move closer. They signal to each other and, sensing the danger, they all run to escape.

**Howler monkeys** live in the thick forest. Because they cannot always see through the leaves, they call out to each other. They make many different kinds of noises by howling, grunting, groaning and gurgling. If one of them finds a good tree in which to sleep, it calls out to tell the others.

**Dolphins** swim together in schools. They talk to each other by making chattering and whistling sounds. If a baby dolphin swims too far away, its mother calls it back to the safety of the group.

Each **badger** group lives in a special place in the forest. This is its territory. Badgers mark out their territory using a special gland in their bodies, because they do not want other groups living too near them. The smell tells other badgers that a group is already living there.

**Gorillas** live in small peaceful groups. They have many ways of telling other groups to keep away from their territory. If two huge males meet, they give each other fierce looks, meaning 'go away'. If this does not work, they roar and bang their chests. The gorillas do not want to fight, so they try to scare off any strangers that come too close to them.

# Hunting for food

By living and working together animals have a better chance of hunting and finding the food they need. This can also be shared by the group.

**Pelicans** help each other to catch fish. A group forms a horseshoe shape. As the pelicans move forwards, they beat their wings on the water. They drive the fish to shallow water where the pelicans catch them.

**Killer whales** hunt in packs of six or seven. They attack huge right whales. They chase the whale until it is tired out and then share the meal.

**Cattle egrets** work together. Some of the birds beat the grass with their wings. Others behind them catch the insects that have been disturbed. The egrets then change places.

**Jackals** live in family groups, but many families join together in packs to hunt large animals. While some of the jackals hunt, others stay behind to look after the cubs. The food is brought back and shared by all the jackals.

**Lionesses** do most of the hunting for their group, called a pride. They hunt as a team. They catch more food for the pride because they work together.

# Caring for each other

Some animals in large groups take great care of each other. They look after the young, the old, the sick and the injured.

**Monkeys** search each other's fur for dirt and fleas. This is called grooming. Although they do not always have fleas, monkeys enjoy being groomed. It shows friendship and care for one another.

**Whales** travel in large groups called schools. If one of them is sick or hurt, the whales will not leave it. They try to help the sick animal even if it is dangerous to do so.

**Zebras** live in family groups which all belong to a large herd. The family is made up of a male with up to ten females and their young. All the animals in the herd care for each other. If one zebra strays away from the herd, the others search for it until it is found.

All the females in an **elephant** herd share in caring for the young. The males watch over the whole herd. If an animal is injured while the herd is on the move, the males support it between them and help it along.

# Thousands together

Some insects live together in very large groups. They help each other with the work that needs to be done.

## Ants

Some **ants** build nests on the ground made of earth and dead leaves. Thousands of ants live in the colony.

These ants help each other to carry a leaf back to the nest. It will be used to repair a hole.

Ants know each other by smell. If a strange ant comes to the nest, workers drive it away.

**Amazon ants** attack the nests of **black ants** in armies. They steal the young which they use as slaves. The slaves have to build the nest and feed all the Amazon ants.

# Termites

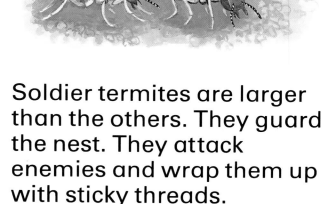

The queen **termite** grows into a long sausage shape. She is full of eggs and cannot move about. Workers swarm over her, carrying away her eggs.

Soldier termites are larger than the others. They guard the nest. They attack enemies and wrap them up with sticky threads.

# Wasps

Some **wasps** build a nest with paper. They scrape wood from trees and chew it into a pulp using their powerful jaws. Inside the nest there are many rooms called cells. The queen wasp lays eggs in these cells.

# Bees

Inside their nest in a hollow tree worker **honey bees** share all the work. They change jobs as they grow older.

cleaning cells

nursing young

finding food

guarding the nest

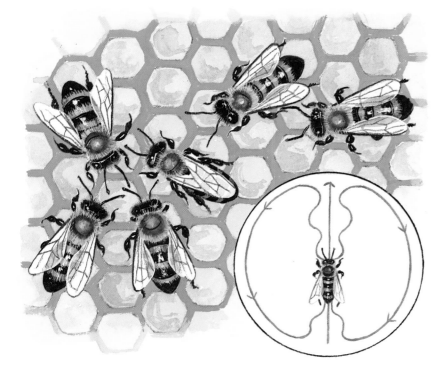

When worker honey bees find some new flowers they return to the nest and dance. As they twist and turn the dance shows the others how far away the flowers are and in which direction the bees must go.

# On the move – for food

Animals make long journeys by land, sea and air. This is called migration. These animals migrate in search of food.

Twice a year in North America, **caribou** travel hundreds of miles. In winter, snow and ice cover their feeding grounds. The herd moves south to find food. They feed there until the spring when mosquitoes begin to hatch. To avoid being bitten, the caribou travel back to the north.

These **wolves** hunt the caribou. When the herd moves, the wolves follow behind. Any caribou that cannot keep up with the herd is overtaken and killed for food.

In Africa there is a wet and a dry season every year. **Wildebeest** live on grass, feeding in small groups during the wet season. In the dry season when there is not enough food, groups of wildebeest gather together in enormous herds. They set off on long journeys in search of better grazing.

Arctic

Mexico

In the summer, **grey whales** feed in the Arctic Ocean. They feed on krill (small shrimps) and they grow very fat. In winter, the sea gets colder so the krill swim down to the sea-bed to escape the cold. Whales cannot feed in such deep waters. They must swim thousands of miles to find food in the warmer seas around Mexico.

# Some animals migrate because of overcrowding.

When the weather is good and there is plenty of food, **locusts** have so many babies that there may be too many of them in one place. A swarm of thousands of babies moves off in search of food. The swarm flies down and strips off the leaves from any growing plant they see.

In winter, **lemmings** shelter underground. They tunnel under the snow eating the roots and stems of plants. The plants cannot grow so there will not be enough food for them all in summer. Thousands of them migrate to new places crossing rivers and streams as they go.

# On the move – to breed

Some animals gather in groups and migrate many thousands of miles to find the best place to have a family. When animals have young, it is called breeding.

Baby **salmon** are born in freshwater streams. When they are old enough, they swim many miles to the sea. Here they feed and grow. A few years later, the adult salmon make the long journey back up the rivers to the same stream in which they were born. Here they lay their eggs.

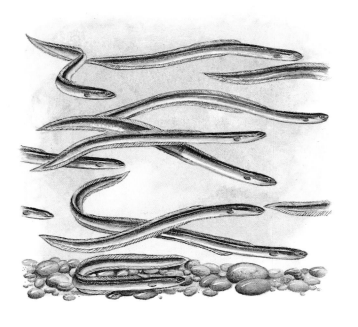

**Eels** live in rivers, but they swim thousands of miles to breed in the sea. The eels lay their eggs in seaweed. The babies, called elvers, take three years to swim back to the rivers where their parents lived.

**Monarch butterflies** live alone in summer. When winter comes, thousands of butterflies gather in huge crowds. They fly south to breed in the warm weather. On their journey they rest in trees at night, using the same trees every year.

North Pole

South Pole

The **Arctic tern** spends the winter at the South Pole. When spring comes, it flies to the other side of the world. The tern nests and has its young at the North Pole where there is plenty of food for its chicks.

**Spiny lobsters** live in shallow water. They migrate to deep waters to lay their eggs. When they travel, the lobsters stay together. They follow each other in a long line.

**Green turtles** travel thousands of miles across oceans to lay their eggs. The turtles gather in large colonies near the shores of small islands. The females leave the sea to lay their eggs on the beach. Then they return to the sea and swim back to their feeding grounds.

# Sleeping in winter

Winter is a difficult time for many animals. Some of them hide away and sleep through this cold time. This is called hibernation.

**Ladybirds** or **ladybugs** escape from the cold by gathering in trees or cracks in rocks. They sleep close together for warmth.

**Horseshoe bats** feed at night catching insects. In winter there are not many insects to catch, so the bats sleep. They hang upside down from a cave roof holding on with their claws.

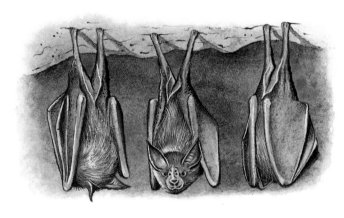

When winter comes, **rattlesnakes** hibernate in large groups. The snakes follow each other's trails to holes or burrows that they use every year. They huddle together, curling round one another.

# Keeping warm

It is important for animals to keep warm.
Some of them do this by staying very close to
each other at different times.

Many birds like these **rooks** gather together in the treetops at night. This is called roosting.

These **bearded reedlings** shelter from the wind in reed beds. They spend the cold nights huddled together for warmth.

These **walruses** live in the cold north. They sleep on top of each other on the beach. There may be thousands of them on one beach.

# Living together

Sometimes different kinds of animals live together.

**Black garden ants** live with **aphids**. The aphids make a sweet liquid that the ants like to eat. The ants take great care of the aphids. They give them shelter in bad weather, look after their eggs and protect them from enemies.

remora

**Remoras** are tiny fish that live with **sharks**. They fix on to the shark's body using a special sucker. They feed on tiny animals that live on the shark's skin. They also eat scraps of the shark's food when it is feeding.

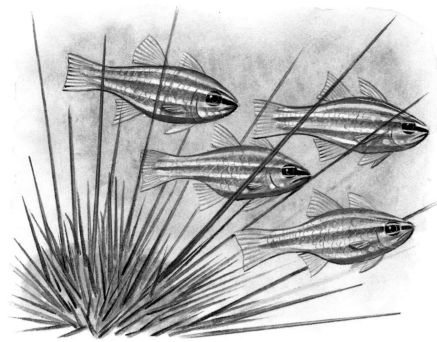

**Cardinal fish** and **sea urchins** live together in the warm Indian Ocean. In the daytime the fish shelter in the sea urchin's long, sharp spines. They eat small scraps of food that are stuck in the spines.

A **hermit crab** often has two other animals living with it. A tiny **bristle worm** hides inside the crab's shell and a **sea anemone** rides on top of the shell. The anemone's stinging tentacles protect all the animals. The crab is a messy feeder and the others feed on scraps of its food.

Animals must find food and protect themselves to stay alive. Some can do this living alone but many others can only survive by living together.